Building Wealth Through Real Estate

It's an attainable goal — and makes sense as part of
a balanced strategy

Lisa Lundt & Team

LISA LUNDT & TEAM

CONTENTS

CHAPTER 1

WHO THIS BOOK IS FOR

When you think of a real estate investor, what picture pops into your mind? You might think of a property developer who buys up lots and builds houses or condos or apartment buildings. You might think of a single family home builder building homes to sell homeowners and landlords. Or the owner of commercial properties which rent space to businesses or medical offices or retail spaces or restaurants. Maybe you know about the investment groups who buy up properties to earn money for their investors. Do you think of yourself? If you don't, you should. Owning real estate is one of the best ways for someone to both earn income and create wealth through the building of equity. It's not a get rich quick scheme, but a deliberate investment strategy. Traditionally, home ownership has been viewed as a sound strategy, earning equity in the home in which you live. Owning a home didn't indicate wealth, but it could act as a different kind of savings account with a good pay out after years of deposits. Of course, you don't have to be a home owner to own real estate. You may live in a place where home ownership doesn't necessarily make sense. If your job requires relocation, you may not want to be tied down to a house, unless you can turn that property into an income producing investment when you do have to move. Every community has a point at which owning makes more sense than renting and it varies significantly from place to place. For instance, if you plan to live in Las Vegas for longer than a year and a half, it makes more sense to buy than rent. However, in Seattle, that time frame is seven years.

Let me tell you about some real estate investors we know. My aunt sold a small apartment building in southern California and wanted to protect some of the profit from taxes through a 1031 exchange. Briefly, a 1031 exchange allows you to take the profit from the sale of something and defer paying the capital gain on the profit by reinvesting the profit into a "like" property; real estate, an airplane, etc. She was less concerned about the equity she would be earning in the property and much more interested in the monthly income she could earn. As it turned out, she bought two properties in Las Vegas in 2008, at the top of the market. The properties are not worth what she paid for them now, but she has been earning a good monthly income, which was her goal and she has no need to sell them anytime soon.

Gary and Linda bought two houses at the bottom of the market when they realized their liquid capital was actually losing money in the bank. Just based upon the monthly income the houses generate they are grossing about 10 percent a month on their investment, plus they are also realizing equity building, increasing the amount of their capital investment at the same time.

Barrett and Katie moved to Las Vegas in 2006 and bought a house at the top of the market. Barrett's a math teacher, so he understands numbers. When he saw how low house prices had fallen, he and Katie took the opportunity to buy not one, not, two, not three, not four, not five, not six, but seven other houses over the years since they arrived here. They've leveraged their first house, by making it income producing and are happily living in a brand new house, while renting out the others and taking advantage of both the income they produce and the equity they are building

Steve is a little more, shall we say, inventive than others. He started out flipping houses by buying properties which needed improvements and selling them for a profit. He wasn't looking for big returns on individual properties, but at least a solid 12 to 15 percent net return on each sale. He was still making more than he would have on any other investment. Not a buy and hold guy, when flipping ceased to be lucrative in one area, he would turn to another. When flipping ceased to be a lucrative investment strategy, he turned to other avenues, such as tax auctions and other avenues. The purchase prices were extremely low, so he could afford to deal with the risks attached to these less traditional real estate investments. Steve uses cash to buy his way into deals and keeps his expectations realistic since his strategy is less about income and more about profit.

Do you see yourself as any of these

people? If so, then this book is for you.

How to Use This Book

When I was in college, I used to read the preface and the last chapter and the bibliography of the books I was reading so I knew what the author wanted me to know and what position he took. Then I would read the book (or most of it) to see how he got to his position. Of course, I was reading the book to either study for a test or use it as a source for a research paper. Don't feel you have to read this book from cover to cover. Think of this book as more of an assistant, to help you turn real estate investment into part of your investment portfolio and as a wealth building strategy.

CHAPTER 2

WHY INVEST IN REAL ESTATE?

Real estate has long been viewed as a wise investment that can help build wealth and future security. Real estate investors come in all sizes, from the home owner who moved up and kept their old home as a rental to the part-time investor who buys a few properties a year to flip, to billionaires owning hundreds of properties. Unlike stocks and bonds, which merely represent ownership in a fraction of a company or a promise to pay interest for money loaned, real estate is backed by something tangible; i.e. the property itself. The value of a property may plummet, but it will always retain some value, unlike stocks in defunct companies.

Our nation recently experienced one of the most devastating recessions since the Great Depression of the 1930's. A combination of factors, including unbridled real estate speculative buying and careless mortgage lending contributed to the financial collapse. Property values plummeted to the point where a large number of them could not be sold for the same amount of money that was owed on the mortgages taken out on them. Other economic factors led to many property owners losing the income needed to pay for these mortgages, and a large number of owners found themselves defaulting on their loans and creating a vast inventory of distressed properties; short sales, foreclosures and auction.

Lenders that had been so loose with their loan requirements suddenly tightened these requirements to the point where it was difficult for potential borrowers to qualify for mortgages. This had the effect of reducing the number of potential buyers quite significantly. Cash became king, with buyers offering cash receiving preference over those making offers contingent on qualifying for loans. Investors with access to cash became the dominant buyers of the plentiful inventory of distressed homes.

As investors snapped up these deeply-discounted distressed properties, prices started rising. Property owners who didn't need to sell their holdings due to financial hardship began putting their houses on the market in order to capitalize on the increasing interest. Public confidence in the economy began rising, and an increasing number of non-investor homebuyers began entering the market, further feeding the real estate market recovery.

Those investors who were bold enough to take a chance on those early years when property prices were at historic lows have obviously profited handsomely for their acceptance of risk. Prices have increased dramatically, although they still have not returned to the historic highs of 2006 and 2007. Interest in real estate is high, with a larger number of homebuyers entering the market.

Despite the fact that property values plummeted during these recessionary times, the fact remains that there was ALWAYS at least SOME value to the real estate. It never completely lost all value. Unlike other durable investments such as collectible vehicles and art, real estate is a necessity of life for the majority of people. Whether someone owns his/her home or rents, the proverbial roof over one's head depends on real estate. We can't say the same for mutual funds and Fortune 500 stocks, which are tools many people believe are necessary for building wealth.

Although most people think about buying and selling real estate for profit, rentals can provide an ongoing cash flow for investors who are prepared for the special requirements of this type of investment. The pool of renters has increased dramatically. Owners who lost their homes during the mortgage crisis are not returning to home ownership at the rate we expected despite changes in lending requirements that shorten the time borrowers have to wait from the time they default on one home loan (whether by foreclosure or short sale) and when they qualify for another loan. These former home owners seem hesitant to jump back into home ownership, preferring to rent.

Younger people are not as eager as their parents at the same age to jump into home ownership either. This demographic age group, often called Millennials, are a perfect target for investors. They tend to be under-employed and unable to bear the financial burdens inherent in home ownership. In addition, this generation simply does not see the value of owning their homes at this time in their lives. As a group, Millennials tend to value the mobility that renting offers. Townhouse and condominium communities may very well experience a renaissance of sorts as younger renters seek out housing that requires little maintenance, offers amenities and is centrally located to work, shopping and entertainment.

The Millennials are the first generation in many decades that places less value in home ownership. The "American

Dream" of owning one's home is actually a fairly recent development, springing up after World War II to capitalize on returning soldiers seeking homes. In other countries, such as Germany, home ownership is not seen as the necessity that many in the United States see it. In these countries, renting is the norm and home ownership is not viewed as offering personal financial security. Although it is impossible to predict the future, the Millennials may be the vanguard of a new attitude towards home ownership as being more of a hindrance than a source of security. Indeed, it is a good time to be an investor!

Although many investors might think

that the best opportunity to make handsome profits in real estate has passed, this simply isn't true. It might take more time to locate properties where the numbers work, but with prices still edging upwards, buyer interest still keen and the potential tenant pool still strong, there is plenty of profit to be made in real estate!

If you are still wondering if investing in real estate is right for you, call us at, or text **ISITRIGHT** to, (877) 413-2660.

CHAPTER 3

MANAGING EXPECTATIONS

Late night television is populated by hosts of "get rich quick on real estate" programs that promise fabulous wealth, but many of these infomercials fail to acknowledge that there is no such thing as free real estate. Financial resources are needed not only to purchase the property (such as cash to cover the entire purchase price, or cash for down payments plus financed funds to pay the balance) but also to pay expenses beyond the actual purchase of the property; closing costs, repairs if necessary, property insurance and for the monthly payment if the purchase is financed are just a few of the expenses of doing business. For investors of rental properties, additional expenses might include those surrounding securing tenants and ongoing/unforeseen repairs, costs of eviction, etc.

Successful real estate investors not only have financial resources, but they have the ability to separate emotionally from their investments. Many new investors make the mistake of getting caught up in the excitement of the purchase and end up paying more for a property than they should. Investing is a numbers game with no room for emotion; a property can be a great investment at one price, but a bad decision at a higher price. The successful investors know that purchases are worth their purchase prices only if the numbers work out, whether those numbers be for a property purchased to resell or one purchased as a rental or long-term investment.

Rental real estate investing has additional requirements, regardless of whether one self-manages or utilizes the services of a property manager. Each state has its own tenant/landlord regulations, and the successful investor needs to know exactly what these are in order to operate within the law. Since rentals tend to involve ongoing relationships with others, whether they be tenants, managers, HOAs, etc it is imperative that the investor be able to keep in fair but firm contact with the parties involved.

As with any form of investment, there is risk involved in real estate. However, with the right team and a bit of homework, much of which you can rely on your team to provide, the payoff should be well worth the risk!

If you are interested in investing in a specific neighborhood and want valuable information to help make an informed decision, visit http://myhousepage.com/where-should-i-invest

CHAPTER 4

DEVELOPING AN INVESTMENT TEAM

Real estate investing is a team effort, with the investor as team captain. There are suitable properties to be located, financing to be arranged (unless cash reserves are available), repairs to be made, tenants to be managed. Although it is possible for the investor to perform all these roles, most find that engaging the services of professionals in their particular fields is not only time saving but money saving as well.

The first step in the vast majority of investment real estate transactions is locating a suitable property. Although some investors find these properties themselves, the majority utilize the services of Realtors. It is vital to choose a Realtor who has experience working with investors. Buyers purchasing homes they intend on living in tend to look at properties differently than investors. These buyers are often seeking homes that are extensions of themselves, and much emotion is wrapped up in their purchases. A Realtor representing such a buyer must be able to help translate these intangible wants and desires into home features that will appeal to the client. Investors, on the other hand, are interested purely in numbers; how will a property purchased at a given price yield a desirable financial gain. A Realtor who excels at helping home buyers find their dream homes may not have the skills required in locating suitable investment properties.

Finding an experienced investment real estate agent may take some research and footwork. Turning to the Internet and calling local real estate offices asking for the names of experienced Realtors will likely yield a long list of prospects. It is advisable to contact the prospects to determine if their experience level is suitable. Questions to ask might include "How many investors do you work with?" "How many investor deals do you close every year?" "Do you work primarily with investors who resell, or with investors who purchase rentals?" In-person interviews with prospective Realtors are also advisable, to assure that both parties are compatible.

Utilizing a Realtor in brokering sales of real estate also offers the buyer (and seller) certain legal protections. Realtors have knowledge of the legal requirements of buying and selling real estate, and can protect their clients by assuring that the transactions meet these requirements.

Many investors bypass Realtors and locate properties themselves. These investors attempt to purchase properties, usually from homeowners who need or want a quick sale, before the homeowner engages the services of Realtors. This is often a favorite method outlined by the late-night get-rich-on-real-estate programs. Although posting "we will by your house" signs on street corners may yield a lot of phone calls, very few will actually result in a purchase, and the investor could possibly be opening him- or herself up to legal issues that would require an additional team member; a lawyer. When it comes to purchasing properties, a Realtor generally costs the buyer nothing to engage his or her services, and for that price is one of the best deals the investor will find.

For investors who purchase rental properties, a major question is whether to self manage or to engage a management company.

Self management has several advantages. There are no management fees to pay, and the owner is free to comparison shop for the best price on repairs and maintenance. The owner also has the opportunity to get to know the tenants, which can go a long way in creating a smooth landlord/tenant relationship. Although self management is generally practiced when the owner lives near his or her investments, it is possible to manage one's own properties from a distance. We have several investor clients who manage their properties from out of state. They have home warranties in place, and tenants call the home warranty company directly to arrange for repairs. One plus to this type of arrangement is that the out-of-area owner can enjoy the opportunity to visit Las Vegas periodically to check up on their properties.

Self management can also be very demanding; being available for phone calls from tenants and arranging required services can be very time-consuming. This option is generally practical for investors with a small number of rentals. Remember our young investors, Barrett and Katie? Katie's job is to manage their properties. This may well be a new career for you, as well.

Engaging the services of a property manager frees owners from the hassle of dealing with the day-to-day issues. Managers act as a buffer between the tenants and the owners; tenants have little if any direct contact with owners. Many management companies have established relationships with repair personnel, and can dispatch them quickly when needed. Fees are generally low, so this buffering function can be quite cost-effective for owners who want to keep distance between themselves and their tenants.

However, it should be made clear that these fees are for that buffering service only; any repairs and evictions are paid for by the owner, with fees for arranging the services added in. When listening to owners discussing property managers, it becomes apparent very quickly that finding a reliable, trustworthy company is difficult. Stories abound of over-priced services and services promised but not delivered. Referrals are the best way of finding a reliable management company. This is also another place where an experienced Realtor may be of assistance.

If an investor is self-managing, he or she will also need to find contractors to provide repair and maintenance services, especially since there are legal requirements to utilize the services of licensed general contractors if repairs exceed certain amounts. It helps immensely to have plumbers, electricians and general repair contacts already lined up. Again, referrals from a Realtor or other sources can meet these needs.

There are three more vital team members who may never see the investments but who are important nonetheless. A lawyer can advise the investor on the best business structure in which to operate. A corporate structure such as a Limited Liability Corporation provide a level of protection between the investor's personal property and any liability that might be incurred by his or her investment efforts. Although the LLC is perhaps one of the most common corporate structures used by real estate investors, there are other options as well, and a good lawyer can advise on the best form to set up.

A good accountant will help the investor navigate through the complex tax laws that govern real estate, and an insurance agent will make sure that the investor is adequately covered against liability, regardless of whether the properties are rentals or resales.

The biggest factor in assembling a great team is trust. The real estate investor needs to find members whom s/he can trust. Communication is critical; team members needs to know exactly what is expected of them so they can perform their function to their maximum capability.

If you need help assembling your team, call us at, or text **TEAM** to, (877) 413-2660.

CHAPTER 5

ACQUIRING PROPERTIES

Now that the primary groundwork is in place, the next step is to determine what kind of housing one wants to purchase. There are three basic categories; single family, attached (condominiums and townhouses) and multiple family (3 & 4 plexes & more.) Depending on one's investment goals and market conditions, one type of property may have advantages over the others. In addition, an investor's real estate portfolio can be a diverse blend of these different properties, much as a well-balanced stock portfolio combines holdings from different sources.

Single family housing is perhaps the most popular category, and the most in demand both for resale and rental. This demand is their strongest asset. Another positive is that it's possible to find properties that do not exist within the control of homeowners' associations and therefore are not subject to monthly HOA fees. The disadvantage is that the owner generally bears the full cost of all maintenance and repair. In some communities under the control of homeowners associations, the HOA may provide certain landscape maintenance functions.

Attached housing, as we mentioned earlier, may experience a renaissance due to the Millennial generation's preference for low maintenance, compact communities that offer amenities and proximity to work, shopping and entertainment. A major advantage to attached housing is that prices per square foot tend to be less than for single family homes. Another advantage is that the HOA generally provides a level of exterior repair and maintenance, relieving the investor of having to cover these costs if they are necessary. Many of these communities offer amenities such as fitness centers, pools, etc. that potential owners and tenants find attractive. One downside is that HOA fees are unavoidable and become an ongoing expense that must be factored into the costs. Some communities do not allow rentals. For those that DO allow rentals, owners are generally responsible for tenants' adherence to community rules, which may include penalty fees for violations. This type of housing is not as much in demand as single family housing and therefore may take longer to sell. However, the popularity of attached housing may be increasing.

Multiple family housing is primarily a rental investor vehicle. They generally offer investors a lower per-unit rate;

for example, the cost of purchasing a 4-plex is generally less than purchasing four similarly-sized single family or attached properties in the same area. Maintenance and repairs are compacted into one area, which can lower costs. The primary disadvantage is that the market for this type of housing is quite specialized, and selling such a property may take a long time. In addition, they are going out of fashion as far as new building projects are concerned because they are expensive to build and aren't seen as the best use of residential land.

Once one has an idea of the type of property to purchase, the next step is to decide if one wants to flip their purchase or hold it as a rental.

Flipping, or buying and selling, is one of the most popular methods of profiting from real estate. The goal is to purchase a property below market value and resell it for a profit. When a market is rising, sometimes all it takes is purchasing a property and holding onto it long enough for values to go up. Generally speaking though, most properties priced low enough to make profit possible require a certain level of repairs prior to placing them on the market. One must factor in these costs plus the costs associated with holding the property for a period of time (such as HOA fees, interest on the mortgage, etc.) into the sale price.

Unlike flipping, which when done correctly generally offers a fairly short-term larger payoff, rentals offer long-term income with the added benefit of appreciation of the property itself. Although rentals can provide steady income, they also incur ongoing expenses and liabilities.

Location may be important if the investor plans on self-managing a rental, but is also important for salability. Size is an important factor as well. Most investors favor 3 bedroom/2 bath or larger as this size home is the most popular one sought by home buyers and renters. For investors who purchase rentals, rentability is a major factor which, as touched on above, can depend on size and location. Although location, size and rentability are important criteria, the bottom line in determining if a property is a worthy investment can be found by doing a little math. A property that may not meet a particular criteria can still be a good deal if the numbers work out!

This is where having an experienced Realtor on the team can be invaluable. A Realtor who is knowledgeable about investment real estate can help locate possible purchases as well as provide data to determine if properties are good deals. If you need help finding investment properties, call us at, or text **INVEST** to, (877) 413-2660.

CHAPTER 6

CASH OR FINANCE

Real Estate is an asset that an investor must pay for and contrary to what the late night infomercials say, there is no such thing as a free piece of real estate. As a result, one of the most important aspects of real estate investing and completing the purchase of a piece of property is understanding the role of financing.

There are basically three general ways

to finance the purchase of an investment property. The first is to pay cash, the second is to borrow or leverage the purchase, and the third is to form some type of partnership to raise the funds.

Cash

Many real estate investors pay cash for their investment properties. Traditionally, approximately 25% of investors in the US paid all cash for their real estate investment and since 2007, this percentage has risen to over 50% in some local areas like Las Vegas, NV.   An all cash transaction is typically the easiest form of financing a purchase as there is no lender complication. While the investor assumes no financing risk in a cash transaction, the return on the investment is typically less than if the transaction were financed with a loan.

For example, if the investor purchased a home for $100,000 and could rent it for $1,000 a month, the annual return would be $12,000 assuming that there were no other expenses. The rate of return on the investment would be 12%.

Conventional Loans

Now assume that the investor could pay 20% down payment on five similar homes that he purchased for $100,000 each and borrow the balance of the funds, i.e., $400,000 to complete the purchase. Let us further assume that the interest rate on the 30 year loans average 5%. The total payment would be approximately $2150 per month or $25,800 per year. Using the same rental rate of $1,000 per home would give a monthly income of $5,000 or an annual income of $60,000 for all five homes. The net income would be $34,200 ($60,000 − 25,800 = $34,200) which would give a return on investment of 34.2% ($34,200/$100,000 = 34.2%).

As you can see, borrowing a portion of the purchase price can significantly improve the return on investment (ROI) for the real estate investor. While many loan programs are available in the financing market today, the most common type of mortgage available to the real estate investor is the conventional loan which typically provides the lowest interest rate when compared to other types of loans.

Conventional mortgage loans may originate from many sources such as mortgage brokers, banks, and credit unions. These lenders are not typically using their own deposits to fund the loan but are using funds from another source. That is to say, these lenders are relying on government backed institutions such as the Federal Home

Loan Mortgage Corporation (Freddie Mac) or the Federal National Mortgage Association (FNMA) or Fannie Mae and or the secondary mortgage market on Wall Street to provide the funds for the loans. As a result, most lending real estate lending institutions underwrite real estate loans based on the guidelines established by Freddie Mac and/or Fannie Mae. These underwriting guidelines may make conventional financing difficult to obtain for many borrowers, especially for real estate investors and other self-employed borrowers.

However, some credit unions and banks have the ability to make real estate loans from their own funds, which makes them a "portfolio lender". Because the loan funds come from their own deposits, they are able to provide more flexible loan term and under-writing standards. This means that they are able to make loans available to real estate investors under terms that are acceptable to that particular lender. Often the results is that the portfolio lender well have real estate loans available with less restrictive underwriting standards than conventional lenders that rely on Freddie Mac or Fannie Mae or the secondary mortgage market as a source of funds. A real estate investor can find these portfolio lenders through referrals from other real estate professionals such as a Realtor.

FHA Loan

The Federal Housing Administration (FHA) is a government program that insures mortgage loans for banks, credit unions, and other lenders. FHA insured loans are designed only for homeowners who are going to live in the property as their primary residence. There is an exception however. FHA will insure a loan on a multi-family loan of a complex up to four units as long as the owner lives in one of the units.

One of the features of an FHA insured loan is that the down payment is as low as 3.5%. This low down payment requirement allows the investor with limited cash reserves to purchase an investment property. FHA also has a program that allows the real estate investor to purchase up to a four unit property that needs repairs and/or improvements as long as one of the units is occupied by the owner. This program is called the 203K Loan Program. The 203K Loan Program also allows for the low down payment of 3/5%.

Fannie Mae's HomePath Loan

The HomePath Mortgage is a Fannie Mae loan available to real estate investors (and other home buyers) in an attempt to help sell Fannie Mae's foreclosed properties. Like the FHA loan, the Home Path program allows for a smaller down payment (usually 10%) but unlike the FHA loan, there is no mortgage insurance fee and the loan is available to real estate investors and other non-owner occupied properties. Also, the HomePath loan program includes a feature that allows the financing of repairs and improvements to the property. These loans are only available to purchasers of Fannie Mae owned properties.

Owner Financing

In addition to Mortgage Companies, Banks, and Credit Unions that can finance the purchase of real estate for the investor, the owner of the property can also finance the purchase for the new buyer. Usually, the seller that finances the property has no existing loan on the property (the property is owned by the seller "free and clear"). In this example, the buyer would make the payments to the seller of the property and not to a bank or mortgage company.

The buyer or real estate investor needs to be cautions of this type of transaction. Many loans have a "due on sale" clause in the deed of trust (security instrument that is filed as a lien on the property). If the property is sold, the loan become could become immediately due in full at the time of the sale. That is to say, if the loan is not paid at the time of the sale, the entire balance of the loan could become due and payable to the lender. If the seller has an existing loan on the property at the time of the sale to the real estate investor, there is a substantial risk that the existing lender could foreclose on the property if and when they find out about the sale.

Hard Money Lenders

Hard Money Financing is obtained from

private business or individuals typically for the purpose of short term investing in real estate. These types of loans are primarily based on the value of the property and are often written with a term of no longer than 36 months. The terms usually include an interest rate of 10% to 18% with up from "point" of 3% to 5%. Because to the loan is based primarily on the value of the property, many hard money lenders do not rely on income verification, credit references or reports, financial statements, or other credit information.

Many land developments, construction projects, and real estate "flips" have been financed with hard money loans.

These loans are difficult to obtain since 2007 and many loans are written for no more than 50% of the value or purchase price of the property unless the hard money lender has a successful history with the borrower.

Home Equity Loans and Lines of Credit

Many investors have chosen to use the existing equity of their own primary residence to assist in the financing of purchase of a real estate investment. Many lenders have loan programs designed for this purpose that allow homeowners to borrow on the equity of their home. An example of these programs would include the Home Equity Line of Credit (HELOC) or Home Equity Installment Loan (HEIL).

Partnerships

One of the main advantages of a Partnership is that the group making up the Partnership is able to purchase real estate investments that the individual partners could or would not afford purchase on their own. Another advantage is that the partners are able to spread their risk by investing on a more diverse portfolio of real estate investments under the partnership than they could if they invested on their own. There partnerships may take many different forms which would include, LLCs, Limited Partnerships, General Partnerships, and Sub-S Corporation. The partnerships could employ the financing methods described above by paying cash for the real estate investment or leveraging the purchase through loan funds for a lender.

Commercial Loans

While most of the financing options available to the real estate investor for residential properties with four units or less is focused on individual investor's income, the commercial lender is more focused on the income of the property itself. The results is that Commercial Loans typically carry higher interest rates and fees in addition to shorter terms in addition to different qualifying standards when compared to the underwriting standards for loans made on properties with four units or less. The reasoning behind this is understandable when you consider the size of the commercial loans when compared to residential loans. An individual real estate investor purchasing a home and borrowing $250,000 is much different to a lender than a real estate investor purchasing a $15,000,000 apartment building. The commercial underwriter will still review the personal income, credit, and other personal financial data but will primarily focus on the revenue generated by the property itself. That is to say the primary source of income that will service the debt of the property will come from the property itself and not from the individual owning the property.

The result is that the loan to value ratios on the commercial loans are generally much more conservative than those used to finance residential properties with four units or less. Loan to value ratios maybe closer to 70% rather than 80% with the primary focus on the debt service coverage ratio of the property. That is to say, what is the ability of the income of the property to service (pay for) the monthly payment.

If you need more information on your financial options, call us at, or text **FINANCE** to, (877) 413-2660

CHAPTER 7

TO MANAGE OR NOT TO MANAGE; THAT IS THE QUESTION

Investors who purchase properties as rentals face the dilemma of who will manage their investments. Both methods have their advantages and disadvantages, and the wise investor will balance the pros and cons against his or her own preferences.

Most investors start off managing their

properties themselves. There are no management costs to pay, and investors can choose whatever maintenance and repair companies that they wish. Self management allows the owner to get to know their tenants and develop a working relationship with them, which can go a long way towards identifying potential issues before they become problems. It allows the owner to keep a closer tab on property as s/he is the main contact point for questions and concerns.

The biggest downside to self management is perhaps one of its biggest advantages, and that is the investor is the "go-to" person for every question, complaint and repair request.

If the sewer line backs up at midnight, the investor will be the one getting the call. Self management can be time consuming; unless the owner has an extensive list of maintenance and repair personnel, much time can be spent visiting properties to follow up on complaints and repair requests, locating and scheduling service. It the owner doesn't live in the vicinity of his/her properties, this time element can be dramatically increased by transit times, not to mention transportation expenses. In addition, it can be awkward for an owner who has had a working relationship with a tenant to initiate eviction proceedings should the need arise.

Many investors will either start immediately with property management companies, or engage their services when the time spent self-managing becomes unprofitable or undesirable. A major advantage of property management companies is the convenience they offer as the point of contact for tenants, freeing the owner from the day-to-day issues that may come up. The management fees are usually quite reasonable, and generally are a percentage of monthly rent. When repair or maintenance issues arise, the property management company arranges service.

The biggest down-side of property management is that it can be difficult finding a reliable company. With the dramatic increase in real estate investors, property management companies have cropped up seemingly overnight, and the industry has experienced a lot of negative press due to the large number of companies that are not delivering on their promises.

Although the management fees can be quite reasonable, repair and maintenance fees can be quite costly as the owner is not only paying for the technician, they are also paying for the property management's scheduling services.

If you would like to discuss whether self-management or hiring a property manager is your best option, call us at, or text **MANAGE** to, (877) 413-2660.

CHAPTER 8

FOREIGN INVESTORS

Foreign investors face obstacles in purchasing real estate, but with the right planning and team members, the challenges are quite manageable.

One of the first steps foreign investors must take is to transfer funds for purchase to US banks. In addition to finding an institution that offers the most reasonable fees and monthly charges, it is also vital to find a bank that is accessible from one's own country. Many foreign investors find that institutions with online access work out quite well.

Managing a real estate investment portfolio from outside the country presents unique challenges. Although it is important for ALL investors to assemble the best team for their business, a great team is especially important for foreign investors who will depend upon the members to be their eyes and ears to a greater degree. Thanks to the Internet and the popularity of online communication applications such as Skype, GoToMeeting, etc. it has become a lot easier for foreign investors to put together their teams. It is vital for members to be comfortable using technology to keep in real-time communication. The face-to-face aspect of online communication also allows foreign investors to develop more of a "feel" and level of trust in their team members. Since distance and the ability to easily travel from home base to an investment property is extremely limited, it is important for the investor to trust his or her team members to do their jobs with little to no supervision, often for extended periods of time.

Although local investors are well-served to discuss the formation of protective corporate entities for their investment efforts, this is practically a must for foreign investors. Companies such as Corporate Credibility, LLC assist foreign investors in setting up the correct type of corporation for their specific needs. Different investments are best served by different types of corporations. The country that the investor is from will also help determine the best type of entity. This is vital for the investor's tax liability as well as the security of their investment.

Foreign investors also need to be aware of The Foreign Investment in Real Property Tax Act of 1980 (FIRPTA). FIRPTA is a United States tax law that imposes income tax on foreign persons disposing of United States real property interests. Tax is imposed at regular tax rates for the type of taxpayer on the amount of gain considered recognized. Purchasers of real property interests are required to withhold tax on payment for the property. Withholding may be reduced from the standard 10% to an amount that will cover the tax liability, upon application in advance of sale to the Internal Revenue Service. Because of the FIRPTA implications it is vital for foreign investors to get a US tax ID number and to have an accountant that is familiar with these ramifications in order to reduce the amount of tax that will be paid upon the selling of any properties.

Foreign investors need to make themselves familiar with US real estate laws, especially those that pertain to foreign investments. It is vital that these investors familiarize themselves with the contracts and terminology used in this country, so they understand exactly what they are signing. Having a professional go over the forms with the investor prior to signing is a wise move.

If you want additional information on how foreign investors can take advantage of our dynamic real estate market, call us at, or text **FOREIGNINVEST** to, (877) 413-2660.

WHAT'S YOUR NEXT MOVE?

IF YOU HAVEN'T ALREADY, VISIT HTTP://myhousepage.com/where-should-i-invest for neighborhood information or call me at (702) 401-2349 to evaluate your personal situation and come up with a game plan that will get you to where you want to be.

If you'd like to give a copy of this book to a friend, relative or work association please call (877) 413-2660 or text BOOK to the same number.

ABOUT THE AUTHORS

Lisa Lundt and her husband, Bob, started their real estate careers in real estate investment. After their move to Las Vegas in 2003, Lisa decided to use her knowledge of real estate by becoming a Realtor. Her ability to stay on top of market trends and willingness to share that information, makes her the Las Vegas Home Specialist. It has also made her one of the top 50 most successful short sale agents in Las Vegas.

Bob Brokaw has been in the real estate business over 30 years as a developer and builder and has worked in the banking sector as well. After encouraging wife Lisa to get her real estate license, he liked what she was doing so well that he decided to join her on the Las Vegas Home Specialist Team.

Andy Karpf is a graduate of the University of Florida. He has been a resident of Nevada since 1999 and a licensed real estate agent since 2001. Over the past several years, Andy has devoted much of his career to helping our Veterans attain the dream of home ownership.

www.ingramcontent.com/pod-product-compliance
Lightning Source LLC
Chambersburg PA
CBHW051735170526
45167CB00002B/943